WHAT ON EARTH IS A
Hyrax

?

EDWARD R. RICCIUTI

A BLACKBIRCH PRESS BOOK
WOODBRIDGE, CONNECTICUT

Published by Blackbirch Press, Inc.
260 Amity Road
Woodbridge, Connecticut 06525

©1997 Blackbirch Press, Inc.
First Edition

Printed in the United States of America

10 9 8 7 6 5 4 3 2 1

Photo Credits

Cover, title page: ©Reed/Williams/Animals Animals
Pages 4—5: ©Bruce Davidson/Animals Animals; page 6: ©Tom McHugh/Photo Researchers, Inc.; page 7: ©Patti Murray/Animals Animals; page 9: ©Stephen J. Krasemann/Peter Arnold, Inc.; page 10: ©Patti Murray/Animals Animals; page 11: ©Reed/Williams/Animals Animals; page 12: ©Patti Murray/Animals Animals; page 13: ©Patti Murray/Animals Animals; page 14: ©Patti Murray/Animals Animals; page 15: ©Patti Murray/Animals Animals; pages 16—17: ©David C. Fritts/Animals Animals; page 18: ©Anup and Manoj Shah/Animals Animals; page 19: ©Patti Murray/Animals Animals; pages 20—21. Bruce Davidson/Animals Animals; page 20 (inset): ©Patti Murray/Animals Animals; pages 22—23: ©B. G. Murray, Jr./Animals Animals; page 24: ©Patti Murray/Animals Animals; page 26: ©Anthony Bannister/Animals Animals; page 27: ©Patti Murray/Animals Animals; pages 28—29: ©Anthony Bannister/Animals Animals.
Map by Blackbirch Graphics, Inc.

Library of Congress Cataloging-in-Publication Data

Ricciuti, Edward R.
What on earth is — a hyrax? / by Edward R. Ricciuti. — 1st edition.
   p.   cm. — (What on earth series)
   Includes bibliographical references (p.   ) and index.
   ISBN 1-56711-100-9 (lib. bdg.: alk. paper)
1. Hyraxes—Juvenile literature. [1. Hyraxes. 2. Mammals.]
I. Title. II. Series.
QL737.H9R53 1997
599.6'2—dc20
                          94-36411
                            CIP
                            AC

What does it look like?

Where does it live?

What does it eat?

How does it reproduce?

How does it survive?

TURN THESE PAGES AND FIND OUT!

Hyraxes are rabbit-sized animals with a mysterious past. Scientists once thought hyraxes were rodents, like guinea pigs, mice, rats, and squirrels. Until recently, some scientists even suspected that hyraxes were distantly related to elephants and sea cows. Now, many scientists believe that hyraxes, horses, and rhinoceroses had similar ancestors millions of years ago. The exact truth about hyrax ancestors, however, no one really knows for sure.

MANY SCIENTISTS BELIEVE HYRAXES ARE DISTANT RELATIVES OF HORSES AND RHINOCEROSES.

ROCK HYRAXES ARE ONE OF THE THREE GROUPS OF HYRAX SPECIES.

Hyraxes are mammals, like whales, deer, cats, and humans. Mammals have hair and give birth to live young that feed on their mother's milk. As a group, mammals are what scientists call a "class" of animals. Other classes include birds, reptiles, amphibians, and fishes.

Each class is made up of smaller groups called "orders." Orders are divided into "families." Hyraxes belong to an order and a family all their own. Within their special family there are several kinds, or species, of hyraxes. Most scientists do not agree on the exact number of species, but they believe there are no less than 12. Most scientists divide the species into three groups—rock hyraxes, bush hyraxes, and tree hyraxes.

TREE HYRAXES ARE THE MOST ACTIVE CLIMBERS OF THE THREE GROUPS.

Hyraxes seem to have a way of confusing people, especially when it comes to names. The word *hyrax* is an ancient Greek term, which means "shrew." Shrews and hyraxes, however, are very different animals.

An entire country may even get its name from yet another mistake people made about hyraxes. Three thousand years ago, travelers from the Middle East arrived in southwestern Europe. There, they saw many animals they thought were hyraxes. They named the land "Ishapan," which means "land of the hyraxes." "Ishapan" may be the origin of the name "Spain." The mistake came from the fact that the animals the travelers saw were not hyraxes at all; they were rabbits.

IN THE PAST, HYRAXES HAVE BEEN CONFUSED WITH MANY OTHER ANIMALS, INCLUDING SHREWS, RODENTS, AND EVEN RABBITS.

Depending on the species, hyraxes can weigh between 4 and 10 pounds (1.8 to 4.5 kilograms) and can be 1 to 2 feet (.3 to .6 meter) long. Hyrax fur is made up of two types of hair—a thick, short undercoat of

ABOVE: HYRAXES HAVE LONG FRONT TEETH THAT ARE SHAPED LIKE TUSKS.
OPPOSITE: THE FEET OF A HYRAX HAVE SPECIAL MUSCLES
THAT ENABLE THEM TO ACT AS SUCTION CUPS.

brownish gray, and longer, blackish hairs that are thinly scattered over the body. Hyraxes have long whiskers and long front teeth, or incisors—two on top and four on the bottom. The lower incisors are shaped like chisels, while those on top are curving tusks that stick out below the hyrax's upper lip.

The soles of a hyrax's feet are covered by thick, flexible pads that perspire when it walks or runs. Muscles in a hyrax's foot can lift the center of its sole, so it takes on the shape of a suction cup.

HYRAXES CAN BE FOUND THROUGHOUT AFRICA AND PARTS OF THE MIDDLE EAST.

Europe

Middle East

Africa

Atlantic Ocean

Indian Ocean

WHERE HYRAXES ARE FOUND

Hyraxes live throughout most of the African continent. Rock hyraxes also inhabit parts of the Middle East, in countries such as Israel and Saudi Arabia.

The typical hyrax habitat has a warm climate, even though parts of the Middle East and the African mountains have temperatures that can be quite cold.

The flexible feet of hyraxes are not built for digging, so they do not burrow. Holes in trees and thick clusters of leaves provide shelter for tree hyraxes. Rock and bush hyraxes stay close to boulders and cliffs, where they take cover in crevices and small caves. Their favorite homes are small, rocky hills that dot the open country of Africa. These hills, called *kopjes*, provide hyraxes with shelter, water, and food.

ROCK HYRAXES USE CREVICES IN CLIFFS AS SHELTER AND PROTECTION.

Hyraxes eat plants—mostly grasses—as well as leaves and bark. A hyrax gathers grass with its tongue and then chews with its rear teeth, while moving its head from side to side. Sharp incisors help hyraxes feed on bark. Early in the morning and before sunset are the times hyraxes usually eat. They feed in small groups and sometimes stand on their hind legs to look for food.

A ROCK HYRAX DINES ON SOME CLOVER AND GRASS.

HYRAXES SOMETIMES STAND UP ON THEIR HIND LEGS WHILE SEARCHING FOR FOOD.

A vast number of other animals can inhabit hyrax country, especially in Africa. There are elephants, zebras, wildebeests, antelope, several kinds of wild cats, jackals and wild dogs, baboons, owls, hawks, eagles and storks, snakes and lizards, and even gorillas. Some of these creatures eat hyraxes.

HYENAS OCCASIONALLY
PREY ON HYRAXES.

TO ESCAPE PREDATORS, HYRAXES WILL SQUEEZE INTO SMALL SPACES
WITHIN ROCKS OR CLIFFS.

An animal that eats other animals is called a predator. One of the main predators of hyraxes is a large snake called the rock python. It can enter the holes where hyraxes hide. In the open, eagles, hawks, and owls also feed on hyraxes, as do leopards and smaller wild cats. Jackals, hyenas, wild dogs, and even baboons have also been known to dine on hyraxes. To survive all these enemies, hyraxes must be very wary.

IF CORNERED, A HYRAX WILL USE ITS SHARP TEETH AGAINST AN ENEMY.

While a hyrax group feeds, an adult male or female usually stands as a lookout for predators. If the lookout senses danger, it will whistle, alerting the feeding hyraxes. A louder cry from the lookout, or any other hyrax in the group, will send all of them running for cover. It is difficult for a predator to catch a fleeing

A LONE HYRAX STANDS
GUARD, WATCHING FOR
PREDATORS WHILE
OTHERS FEED.

hyrax. A hyrax's strong legs enable it to run at a
gallop and jump quickly off the ground. The sweaty,
flexible cups on its feet help a hyrax stick to rocks,
so it can scamper up a cliff with ease. If cornered in
its hole, an adult hyrax may grind its teeth, growl,
and fight back with its sharp tusks. Even though they
are small, hyraxes can deliver a nasty bite.

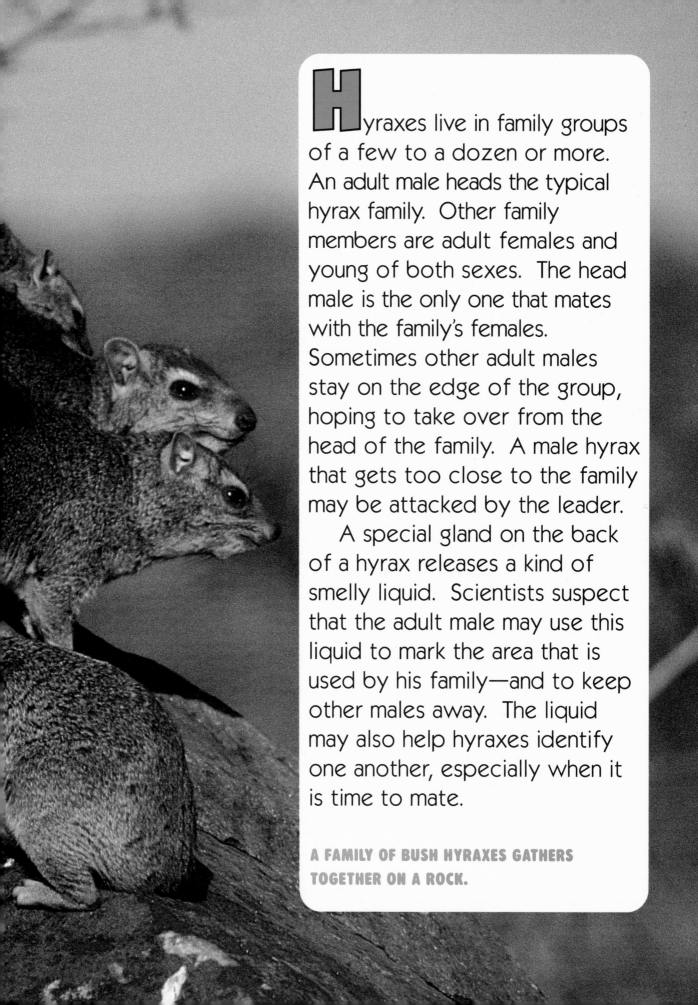

Hyraxes live in family groups of a few to a dozen or more. An adult male heads the typical hyrax family. Other family members are adult females and young of both sexes. The head male is the only one that mates with the family's females. Sometimes other adult males stay on the edge of the group, hoping to take over from the head of the family. A male hyrax that gets too close to the family may be attacked by the leader.

A special gland on the back of a hyrax releases a kind of smelly liquid. Scientists suspect that the adult male may use this liquid to mark the area that is used by his family—and to keep other males away. The liquid may also help hyraxes identify one another, especially when it is time to mate.

A FAMILY OF BUSH HYRAXES GATHERS TOGETHER ON A ROCK.

Most hyraxes mate once a year. The time of year seems to depend on when the rainy season starts. Mating usually takes place during the dry season, which means the young are born about the time the rains begin. This is also the time when the plants that will eventually be needed by the baby hyraxes start to grow.

Hyraxes mate much like other mammals. A male fertilizes the eggs of the female, which causes a new organism to develop. This tiny developing organism is called an embryo. An embryo develops inside the female for about six months before it becomes a hyrax ready to be born.

AS IS TRUE WITH MOST ANIMALS, BOTH MALES AND FEMALES ARE NEEDED IN ORDER
TO REPRODUCE.

A MOTHER SUNS HERSELF ON A ROCK WHILE HER YOUNG STAY CLOSE BY.

The average female hyrax has between one and four young. They weigh about a half pound (.225 grams), look like miniature adults, and can run and jump only a few minutes after they are born! This is an advantage for a young animal that has many predators. Young hyraxes will often climb up on their mothers so liquid from her back gland will stick to their bodies. The liquid's smell helps the mother identify her young.

At first, young hyraxes only feed on milk from their mother. Gradually, they begin to eat plants as well. Within six months, the young feed only on plants and are adult size. By the time they are about a year-and-a-half old, hyraxes are first ready to mate. The newly adult males leave the family or are driven away by the head male. The newly adult females of the family remain.

YOUNG HYRAXES WILL OFTEN CLIMB UP ON THEIR MOTHER'S BACK TO RUB AGAINST A SPECIAL GLAND THAT GIVES THEM A UNIQUE SMELL.

Human activities that threaten many kinds of animals have also reduced the numbers of hyraxes in some regions.

The greatest threat to hyraxes is the destruction of their habitat. Human populations are skyrocketing in regions that are also inhabited by hyraxes. More people in these areas means that more land must be

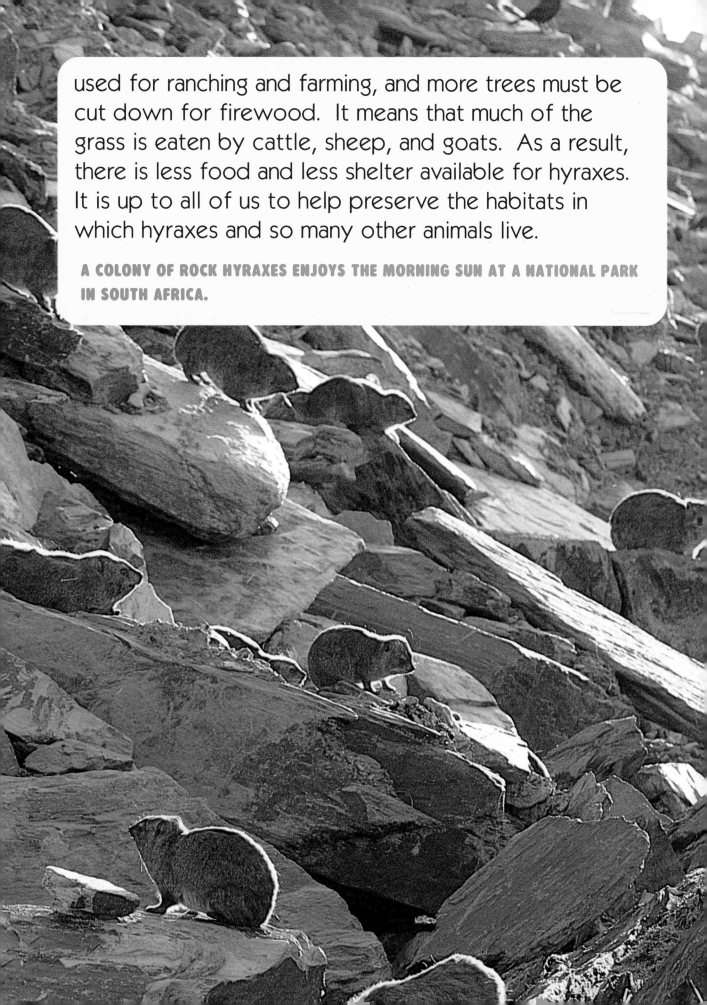

used for ranching and farming, and more trees must be cut down for firewood. It means that much of the grass is eaten by cattle, sheep, and goats. As a result, there is less food and less shelter available for hyraxes. It is up to all of us to help preserve the habitats in which hyraxes and so many other animals live.

A COLONY OF ROCK HYRAXES ENJOYS THE MORNING SUN AT A NATIONAL PARK IN SOUTH AFRICA.

Glossary

hyrax pronunciation: hi•raks

ancestors Ancient relatives.

burrow To dig into the ground.

class A scientific grouping of animals by special characteristics.

egg Female sex cell.

embryo The young organism developing inside the egg.

fertilization The joining of sperm and egg that creates the embryo.

habitat Surroundings that provide an animal with space, shelter, and food.

incisors Upper and lower front teeth.

mammals The group of animals, including people, that produce their own body heat, have hair, and feed their young on mother's milk.

order A grouping or classification of animals that make up a class.

predator An animal that hunts other animals for food.

species A kind of organism within a family of organisms.

tusks Long, sharp upper teeth.

Further Reading

Bargar and Johnson. *Pythons*. Vero Beach, FL:
Rourke Corporation, Inc., 1987.

Baskin-Salzburg, Anita, and Salzberg, Allen.
Predators! Chicago: Watts, 1991.

Ganeri, Anita. *Small Mammals*. Chicago: Watts,
1993.

Georges, D. V. *Africa*. Chicago: Childrens Press,
1986.

Lambert, David. *The Golden Concise Encyclopedia
of Mammals*. New York: Western, 1992.

Parsons, Alexandra. *Amazing Mammals*. New York:
Random House, 1990.

Purcell, John W. *African Animals*. Chicago:
Childrens Press, 1982.

Tesar, Jenny. *Mammals*. Woodbridge, CT:
Blackbirch Press, Inc., 1993.

The Sierra Club Book of Small Mammals. San
Francisco: Sierra, 1993.

Index

Africa, 13, 17

Baboon, 17, 19
Bush hyrax, 7, 13

Eagle, 17, 19

Hawk, 17, 19
Hyena, 19
Hyrax
    defense, 20—21
    embryo, 24
    feet, 11, 13, 21
    food, 14
    fur, 10—11
    gland, 23, 26
    habitat, 13, 28
    legs, 21
    length, 10
    mating, 23, 24
    name, 8
    predators, 19, 20, 26
    teeth (incisors), 11, 14, 21

    tongue, 14
    weight, 10
    whiskers, 11
    young, 26—27

Jackal, 17, 19

Kopjes, 13

Leopard, 19

Middle East, 13

Owl, 17, 19

Rock hyrax, 7, 13
Rock python, 19

Tree hyrax, 7, 13

Wild cats, 17, 19
Wild dogs, 17, 19

j599.6   98-1247

Ricciuti, Edward R.

   What on Earth is a HYRAX?

DATE DUE   1-3

SE 30 '98			
MY 08 '99			
NO 27 '99			